THE JUDITH WILSON LECTURE 1967

SOME UNCONSCIOUS INFLUENCES IN THE THEATRE

BY

ANN JELLICOE

CAMBRIDGE
AT THE UNIVERSITY PRESS

1967

Published by the Syndics of the Cambridge University Press
Bentley House, 200 Euston Road, London, N.W.1
American Branch: 32 East 57th Street, New York, N.Y.10022

© Cambridge University Press 1967

*This Judith Wilson Lecture was delivered in the
University of Cambridge on 10 March 1967*

Printed in Great Britain
at the University Printing House, Cambridge
(Brooke Crutchley, University Printer)

ALL art seeks to impose its own truth, and I want to consider some of the ways in which a dramatist tries to impose his truth upon us, how we are conditioned before ever we enter the theatre, the unconscious and unacknowledged forces operating upon us while we are there, finally I want to consider how the desire to impose truth may defeat itself.

It would be idle to try and define truth except to say that insofar as the artist is concerned truth is his personal view of fact and reality interpreted by him in terms of his art; but it may also be the demand of a work of art to be pursued to its absolute conclusion. The validity of an artist's view and interpretation of truth obviously depends upon his integrity, perception and skill as an artist. I am unwilling to discuss how far the artist's perception of truth may depend upon intellectual intelligence or upon that other artistic intelligence—the intelligence a sculptor may have in his hands for example.

But I would suggest that for most artists creating a work of art is also indissolubly searching for truth; and that art is less a process of creation than a process of discovery: the work demands and creates itself, the artist merely waits attentively for the work to reveal itself. But this also demands that the artist ask certain questions, answer certain problems in seeking to discover the nature of the work. And in his struggle the artist makes discoveries which release energy, excitement and enthusiasm which give his work power. The power of a work springs directly from its truth. The work having been created there is then an urgent desire to show it to other people. Artists must communicate. A work of art is not complete until it reaches its audience.

All art demands its audience but the audience is especially important in the theatre. In the theatre the audience cannot have an individual reaction, and their corporate reaction swamps individual judgement in a manner, and to a degree, I wouldn't have thought possible if I hadn't had the experience of travelling round the provinces on tour with my own play, seeing a familiar work with different audiences, and observing how those audiences affected my judgement of the work. The theatrical experience is not merely the experience of the play, but of experiencing it in company with the rest of the audience who colour the event to a degree of which one is largely unconscious.

But let us go back for the moment and consider one of the reasons why the audience goes to the theatre. The theatre audience is notoriously not a fair cross-section of the population. By and large they are newspaper readers. The theatre-going public is largely the readership of those papers giving most space to theatre criticism. Theatre people will tell you that the *Mirror*, the *News of the World* and *The People* mean little at the box office; but *The Times, Telegraph, Guardian, Financial Times, Express, Mail*, the two London evening papers and the three top Sundays all have great influence. One wants a good notice, or better still, a good selling notice, in any of them.

There is not much to choose between a good notice and a good selling notice, but for those concerned it may mean the difference between a degree of penury and considerable affluence. A good notice may finish by saying: 'There is nothing in this play which need deter the intelligent theatre goer.' A good selling notice may end: 'I urge you to see it.' A subtle degree of enthusiasm, but it means an immense difference in audience numbers. A really enthusiastic set of notices will bring huge audiences, all convinced they are going to see a good play. Whether it is in fact good is almost beside the point. The audience has been authoritatively told it's good, and by and large they will accept it as good; just as if they've been told it's funny they will tend to laugh. People look for what they have been told they will see. More subtly, if Harold Hobson says (as he has said) that Beckett is a greater writer than Sophocles then the audience who read Hobson are going to approach Beckett in a certain state of mind, for it has been strongly suggested that not merely is he a great writer, he is also a classic. It takes an awareness of the process and considerable confidence in one's own judgement to stand out against this conditioning.

More usefully critics will sort out an audience. Peter Lewis says in the *Mail* 'Rich uproarious belly laughs'. Of the same play Phillip Hope-Wallace writes in *The Guardian* 'Somewhat coarse humour'. One audience will be guided to the play, another will stay away. Obviously a certain kind of play will attract a certain kind of audience—intellectual perhaps at the Royal Court, less so at Drury Lane. An audience of common background and common age will react predictably to certain plays. Within the theatre certain factors are important. The business executives, doctors and lawyers in the stalls and dress circle have different values and may react differently from the teachers in the upper circle and the students in the gallery. Working as author or director I have often moved round a theatre during performance and noted that the stalls are indifferent while the balcony is enjoying itself. You will even find small pockets of reaction, their influence spreading for a few seats around and then falling off. The physical shape of a theatre is most important—too vast a subject to consider here; basically if you can't see or hear very well you may not be so deeply involved, unless there is a compensating strong audience reaction to lift you along—what one might call the gallery syndrome.

What does audience reaction mean? How does it work? What is actually happening when the audience reacts? It is a process that is taking place at this moment, for here I am, the performer, my status enhanced by an introduction, a raised position, the nature of the occasion when it is my privilege to speak. This all gives me power. And yet the very steps taken to protect my status imply my insecurity in this role. A process is taking place amongst you, of which you are probably unaware; you think you are forming an individual judgement, but I suggest you are forming a group judgement.

The first time I recognised this phenomenon and was able to isolate it was during the provincial tour of my play *The Knack*. The play opened here in Cambridge and the theatre was filled each night by young people who greatly enjoyed themselves. Without wishing to flatter I would say that undergraduates make good audiences, because the standard of intelligence is high, reactions are quick and lively; undergraduates tend to see a joke just before the point has been reached, thus they give themselves the extra, exquisite pleasure of having their suspicions confirmed. These audiences laughed a great deal and so did I. I watched the play three or four times sitting amongst them and laughed with them. I was aware that I wasn't totally in control of my reactions —self-control is the enemy of good theatre. The play did seem very funny, yet I'd lived with it for a long time and watched it many times in rehearsal, but with those first audiences it seemed quite fresh; I laughed at the play not as if I were seeing it for the first time but with a kind of fresh delight. Someone said to me, 'You laugh at your own play then?' and I had to confess I did; I excused myself by saying that the actors were extremely good—I genuinely did think this was the reason, and indeed the actors were good, but it was not the reason I laughed. The following week the play went to Bath—Bath in the late autumn when most of the summer visitors, such as they were, had departed. The audiences were thin and elderly, they were confused and outraged by the play, it was too quick and off-beat in style for them and they had no point of contact with the characters. Moreover, they found the play obscene; there were outraged letters in the local press about the obscene play which dealt with rape and kangaroo nipples and so forth; they couldn't make head or tail of it. Sitting in the auditorium amongst that audience, I did not want to laugh. More than that, the play appeared obscene to me. I had had a number of arguments with the Lord Chamberlain over certain lines which he had wanted to cut, but after discussion we were allowed to retain some of them. When these lines were said in Bath, and other lines which he had never even questioned, it seemed to me that the Lord Chamberlain was right—they were obscene. I began to think the Lord Chamberlain had a nice feeling for obscenity, but it was unpleasant: I had no wish to be the author of obscenity. There followed a good week in Cardiff. They told me the bar takings were the audience wanted to be, and so they willingly and happily projected their dreams and desires upon this fantasy world. The point is that everyone wants to identify with those whom they feel are better than themselves. But what does 'better' mean? It may be more highly born, richer, more successful or perhaps more honest, more idealistic, more truthful, more courageous; or perhaps may be people whom the audience feel live more intensely and vividly than do the audience in their everyday lives.

These images, which society finds so attractive, may become powerful. They may indeed change the world. For we model ourselves on our chosen images, we begin to talk, dress, act and finally think like them. Jimmy Porter was such an image, James Dean another, Mick Jagger is another. I think it true to say that these helped to mould a generation. I don't think Jimmy Porter and James Dean were imposed upon the audiences of the fifties—and I doubt whether any image could be successfully imposed. It's rather that those who create a successful image recognise or sense some current social fantasy and give it a physical form. In a sense the audience creates the image; they create it to answer their need: the audience needs an image to imitate, upon which to project their imagination. By projection I mean that the audience begins to invest the images with their own fantasies and desires, emotional fears, anxieties and drives.

To give an example of what I mean by projection. Some months ago I was watching the Royal Court Theatre Studio, which was a group of professional actors who met regularly to experiment and extend their range. They were working with masks. There are two main types of mask, the comic and the tragic, and the technique of using them is a little different; here I am referring to the tragic mask. The tragic mask covers the actor's whole face, the face of the mask is expressionless, or rather, when held in the hand, has the expression the maker gave it; thus the actor cannot use the expression of his own face. Nor can he use his voice, for unlike the Greek masks, modern masks have no hole for the mouth; the open mouth of the Greek mask demands enormous proportions of the head and similar building up of the body—kothurni, high headdresses, padding, etc., which in turn is related to the size of Greek theatres. With the modern mask the actor appears utterly impoverished —no facial expression, no voice. He relies almost entirely upon the audience projecting its imagination. I was watching a simple scene between a mask and two speaking characters. The mask had lost the key of a tower in which her lover was imprisoned, the mask tried to get help to find the key, her anxiety was intense, at last someone understood, found the key and gave it back to her. At this point the mask smiled. The impression was so strong that I was jolted and looked more carefully, my identification was still strong enough to make me feel the mask really was smiling, I couldn't believe my eyes; they were indeed not to be believed, my intellect knew perfectly well that that mask was made of papiermâché could not be smiling and yet my imagination projected a smile upon the mask. If imagination can make a rigid mask smile what can it not do? What is the limit of imagination in the theatre?

Another related observation: I was watching *Philoctetes* at the National Theatre and was struck by my reaction to Hercules' bow—at one moment I observed it with a detached professional interest as a well-made stage property, the next, my imagination having been caught, I began to invest it with power, it became a magical object to be handled with care and reverence, so that one was literally drawing in one's breath. This touches upon the central theatrical experience, theatrical dichotomy: you identify with the actor and yet you remain yourself. 'I am Hamlet, Prince of Denmark, yet I am also me sitting here in my seat.'

Theatrical dichotomy is the double experience that is at the heart of all theatre-going. The audience knows they are in a theatre watching a play that is make-believe, it's not really happening. They see before them actors on a stage who pretend to be certain people and pretend to be in a particular, developing situation; the actors invite the audience to join in this make-believe. And, given a good theatrical experience, the audience does indeed enter into the play, it allows itself to be carried away, but for most of the time the audience is well aware of reality. It doesn't lose itself entirely in the fantasy world. A double experience is taking place: the audience is caught up in the play and yet it's also aware that it's part of an audience sitting in a theatre. The audience plays at make-believe and knows that it is playing. If you increase the challenge to belief you also increase theatricality. In *A Midsummer Night's Dream* the dramatist has Oberon say, 'I am invisible and I will overhear their conference.' Oberon remains on stage and the actors behave as if he was not there. The audience then has the fun of seeing Oberon four-square in the scene and yet imagining him as invisible simply because he says he is and the other actors behave as if he is. Theatrical dichotomy is a comedian turning around in the middle of a revue sketch and talking directly to the audience, then going back into the sketch again— the reality conflicts with the play-acting and emphasises the two levels upon which the audience is experiencing. The challenge to belief may become finally so great that it is manifestly absurd—as is the case with the pantomime horse. This is so absurd that it demonstrates very clearly the true nature of theatre—theatre as play.

You can play with reality in this way in the theatre because you start with a self-evident basis of reality: live actors on a stage in front of a live audience. Films and television are essentially mechanical forms and they must first persuade you of reality; they are not real, so they must establish a standard of reality. Films and television are not magical because they can do anything. On film you can change a pine cone into a bag of gold, or make a man disappear—and this will actually happen before an audience's eyes, there is no challenge to the imagination. But in the theatre, as I've seen in pantomime, two thieves liable to be caught in a shop can say: 'Let's put this biscuit tin over our heads and then we'll be invisible, no one will see us.' And the other actors behave as if they cannot see them. It's ridiculous—as if putting a biscuit box on his head would make a man invisible. The audience knows the man is not invisible but enters into the joke that he is. The audience connive with the actors and with each other. They play together and in playing they enter into a particular relationship with the others in the theatre.

The audience goes to the theatre to be moved, to be 'taken out of themselves', to be 'carried away'. The good dramatist knows he must capture their imagination and hold it. To do this he uses any number of means, of which those of least use to him are intellectual. If the audience wants to be carried away the dramatist must induce surrender, so that he doesn't want to appeal to reason: rationalisation, objectivity—these are not states of mind which will help an audience to surrender. No. The appeal in the theatre must be to the senses, emotions and instincts. So we have colour, movement, rhythmical and musical sounds and use of words, and we have appeals to the half conscious and the unconscious: symbols, myths and rituals.

The hypnotic, or perhaps I should say psychedelic, qualities of sight and sound have been known and used in the theatre since earliest times, they have probably a more powerful direct effect upon the audience than any other stimuli, barring imagination. But speaking personally, I've long known of the power of sight and sound and the rules, such as they are, governing their use. On the other hand although my first play *The Sport of my Mad Mother* was built upon myth and ritual, it was written intuitively, I had no conscious idea of the means I was using. It's only in recent years that I've been able to analyse symbolism, myth and ritual, and in the time at my disposal I'd rather concentrate on them.

Symbolism has become a dirty word in the theatre since the war, probably because it was used in connection with the abstract, symbolic theatre of thirties when symbols were made obvious and thrust down people's throats. This symbolic theatre developed as the poets' reply to the commercial theatre of the period which was almost wholly concerned with naturalism, materialism and the superficial display of manners. But symbolic theatre, being born of poets, was literary rather than dramatic. Let me digress and give an example of what

I mean by literary. At one time I was running the Royal Court Theatre's Writers' Group, which met once a week in a free and easy fashion to improvise and allow writers to discover something about acting. One day a woman turned up when we were improvising upon the creation of the world. She didn't much like our attitude to the subject which was fairly tough and anarchic (which also means free and experimental), and said so. It seemed a good thing to let her try out her ideas. She set up a scene in which the Creator (herself) sat in the middle, whilst actors, representing the planets, revolved around her. Arnold Wesker and Edward Bond crouched down and revolved with generous seriousness. Her idea didn't work, not only because of the physical limitations of people but because it was literary concept and not a theatrical concept. Later Arnold Wesker did a mime on the same subject with another girl. She sat inert and he began to mime life into her: he demonstrated each sense and then transferred it to her so that she was first roused and then gradually filled with life. This is a very theatrical concept and was later used in *I'm Talking About Jerusalem*.

The symbolic theatre then, was a literary theatre, and not very good at that. Symbolism came to be equated with a gutless abstract idealism, the kind of play where you don't have character but character types, and where every thought and every action has a wider symbolic application which is intellectualised: that is, made concrete in words so that the appeal is to the brain. But if symbolism is dead, symbols inescapably remain.

A symbol is a condensation of many kinds, and many layers, of experience. A symbol embodies an infinite number of ideas and associations more effectively and more economically than words, partly because a symbol is open-ended—each of us may read something different into a symbol and there is no limit to what we may read. But a symbol is also more effective than words simply because we don't as a rule consciously analyse what it means to us, it appeals subtly and insidiously, not to the brain, but to the less rational, less defined parts of our personality: to our emotions and memories.

A myth almost always embodies and illustrates in concrete form some human condition or confusion or perplexity: some tragedy, or mistake or mishap. Myths are the bodying forth, in stories, in images, of our longing, conflicts and fears, they give shape to the deepest human urges, often to unspoken, archetypal drives which cannot be formulated wholly in words. Myths deal often with urges so deeply rooted in human nature that they relate to our earliest infancy and to the earliest infancy of man, urges which have nothing to do with rational thought, and over which rational thought has little power. A myth speaks directly to the deepest parts of our nature.

One thinks of the myth of Hippolytus, the

virginal young man torn to death by his own horses —horse of course being a sexual symbol. But it's quite possible to discover modern myths. I read recently of a fourteen-year-old girl who took her mother's birth control pills and ate them, putting aspirin in their place. As soon as the imagination begins to work on this story one senses the feeling of the ancient gods at play—a kind of meddling with power, so that any child born as a result should perhaps have remarkable and extreme qualities—be excessively ugly perhaps with some compensating special quality, or be marked out for some particular task.

Ritual is a device we use to give our lives scale and significance, to reassure ourselves as to the importance of our values, to celebrate such values. We create rituals when we wish to strengthen, celebrate or define our common life and common values, or when we want to give ourselves confidence to undertake a certain course of action. A ritual generally takes the form of repeating a pattern of words and gestures which tend to excite us above a normal state of mind. Once this state of mind is induced we are receptive and suggestible and ready for the climax of the rite. At the climax the essential nature of something is changed. As examples of rituals we may think of the mass, the marriage ceremony, the bestowal of diplomas, a coronation, etc. All these follow the same pattern, they reiterate a form of words and gestures inducing a mood of excitement and acceptance, when the audience is sufficiently receptive then the essential nature of something—some person, some relationship—is changed.

I would like to follow a specific example and try to illustrate the points that have already been made: the question of image-making in the theatre, of identification, of the appeal to the unconscious by means of symbolism, myth and ritual, and then I would like to show how all these well-laid schemes designed to seduce the audience may be turned inside-out if the dramatist doggedly pursues his idea of what he conceives to be the truth.

Let me take the story of Little Red Riding Hood, which so far as I know has had little dramatic treatment and is not one of the popular pantomimes. Perhaps we should go over the story briefly so that we may refresh our minds over certain details which may have been long since forgotten.

Once upon a time there was a little girl whose grandmother had given her a little red riding hood. The grandmother lived alone in the middle of a forest and one day Little Red Riding Hood's mother said to her, 'Grandma is ill, take this basket of food and bottle of wine to her, and, when you get into the forest, mind you keep to the path so that you don't lose your way or fall and break the bottle.' So Little Red Riding Hood set off. Once she was well into the wood, a wolf saw her and asked where she was going; when he heard she was on her way to her grandmother the wolf suggested that grandmother might like some of the wild flowers which were growing off the path. So Little Red Riding Hood wandered off the path deeper and deeper into the forest. The wolf hurried off to grandmother's house, gobbled up grandmother, put on her cap and spectacles and climbed into bed. Meanwhile Little Red Riding Hood had got lost and been put on her way by a friendly woodsman. When she arrived at grandmother's cottage she found the door open; inside was the wolf dressed as grandmother and sitting up in bed. 'Oh, Grandmother', said Little Red Riding Hood, 'what big ears you have.' 'All the better to hear you with', said the wolf. 'But grandmother, what big eyes you have.' 'All the better to see you with'. 'Oh, grandmother, what big teeth you have.' 'All the better to eat you with.' And at this the wolf jumped out of bed and ate up Little Red Riding Hood. But the woodsman, coming by to see that Little Red Riding Hood was all right, saw the wolf fast asleep after his meal. The woodsman was just about to kill the wolf when he realised that Little Red Riding Hood and her grandmother had disappeared and it occurred to him that the wolf might have eaten them. He slit open the wolf's belly and out popped Little Riding Hood and her grandmother. Little Red Riding Hood filled up the belly of the wolf with stones so that when he woke up he collapsed and died. And they all went home to mother and Little Red Riding

Hood promised never to wander from the path again.

In *The Forgotten Language* Dr Erich Fromm has analysed the symbolic and unconscious aspects of Little Red Riding Hood. He says: 'The little red riding hood is a symbol of menstruation, the warning "not to leave the path" and "not to fall and break the bottle" is a warning against the danger of sex and losing virginity.' The wolf's tempting Little Red Riding Hood into the deep forest is an attempt to seduce her. Fromm continues: 'The male is portrayed as a ruthless, cunning animal, and the sexual act is described as a cannibalistic act in which the male devours the female. This view is not held by women who like men and enjoy sex. But the hate and prejudice against men are more clearly exhibited at the end of the story...we must remember that woman's superiority consists in her ability to bear children. How, then is the wolf made ridiculous? By showing him attempting to play the part of a pregnant woman having living things in his belly. Little Red Riding Hood puts stones, a symbol of sterility, into his belly and the wolf collapses and dies. His death, according to the primitive law of retaliation, is punishment according to his crime, he is killed by stones, the symbol of sterility, which mock his usurpation of the woman's role.'

Perhaps this analysis explains why Little Red Riding Hood has never been as popular a subject for pantomime as say Cinderella or Aladdin. Putting it mildly, there is no one with whom men and boys might happily identify—the woodsman is a minor figure well off centre, but, more than this, men watching the performance are being asked to support an anti-male diatribe and would resent it. They might not know consciously why they didn't like the play, but they would react against it. In such a case they might well produce rationalisations; they might react by saying the play was boring, ill-constructed, pretentious, stupid—any rational reason would serve. Because, quite frankly, we are very often unaware of the real reasons why we reject something. And this includes drama critics. We may very often have valid, although unconscious, reasons for rejecting something—and I would agree with any man who refused to sit quietly through Red Riding Hood. The difficulty comes when we are unaware of our unconscious reasons for rejecting the play, and start rationalising them into false value judgements. It is really quite beside the point to call a play stupid, dull, boring or pretentious, if the real reason for our dislike lies elsewhere. It may indeed be a bad play objectively speaking. But I now distrust all negative criticism since there are so many subjective reasons why a play may be dismissed—reasons to do with our own nature rather than the nature of the play. The only kind of value judgement I do find myself able to trust is that of an artist who likes some piece of work—because an artist is knowledgeable and perceptive about his art and may be very clear as to why he likes the work. I'm afraid, if he dislikes it, an artist's reasons for dislike may be as subjective as anyone else's.

With Little Red Riding Hood as it stands I see little chance of a commercially successful play. I can imagine a socialist realist lesbian suffragette getting it up for a ladies evening, when it might indeed go with a swing. But if it were given a normal production it would be rejected out of hand because, of course, most drama critics are men.

I have said that art is a process of discovery rather than creation, to be more precise, apart from the vital intuitive leaps which an artist must make, the artist's most important job is to discover the right questions he must ask. Suppose one was becoming intrigued by the story of Little Red Riding Hood, to the point of beginning to write about it, what questions would one be asking oneself?

If you were a T.V. story editor—'The Writer's Best Friend' as, I think it was the Head of B.B.C. Drama said not so long ago—no doubt your question would be, 'How can this material be made more attractive to a general audience?' And surely the answer is not all that difficult. Our story editor will surely say that if the dramatist wants to engage the attention of the men in the audience he must strengthen and build up the character of the woodsman. It might be sufficient to have an opening scene demonstrating the power, skill, intelligence and general charm of the woodsman, and then, only when he is thoroughly established bring in Little Red Riding Hood. Thereafter the woodsman must appear regularly to maintain his hold on the audience's imagination. But I doubt if the story editor would consider that sufficient—the wolf is still too dominantly representing men in a most unflattering light. If you want men and boys to enjoy the play you must create an extra plot—quite as strong and possibly stronger than the present main plot. You might even have to introduce another character—the woodsman's little boy. Possibly the woodsman and the boy would be out to save the forest from spoliation by the wolf on the lines of Batman and Robin. Thus given a real hero, the woodsman, the wolf becomes unquestionably the villain and everyone in the audience can comfortably release their aggression towards him. They are free to hate the wolf and thus release the hate that is in all of them, and us, to some degree.

As regards myth and ritual, there is a text-book example of ritual in Little Red Riding Hood. The form of words in the ritual is established with the first two phrases 'Why grandmother what big ears you have', 'All the better to hear you with'. The form is confirmed in the second two phrases with a slight change of words which keeps the interest fresh and indicates further development. 'Why grandmother what big eyes you have', 'All the better to see you with.' With the third repetition the audience now knows the form of words and feels pleasure partly because it is in the know and so is flattered and put at ease, partly because of the sheer rhythmic seduction of the words, the two repetitions pointing to a third towards which the audience is, so to speak, leaning forward in expectation. The third repetition leads to the climax: 'Why grandmother what big teeth you have', 'All the better to eat you with.' Now the wolf's eating Red Riding Hood is not quite a surprise, because the wolf has already eaten the grandmother: the situation is clearly fraught with interest. The audience will be waiting for the climax, will suspect its nature. The reiteration of the verbal formula builds the tension yet holds back the climax, engendering more and more pleasurable excitement and anticipation. At the climax the excitement is released and the essential nature of something is changed.

As regards myth—myth being, at the moment, so fashionable—we can probably find something mythical in the forest: does it not represent the female principle—dark, secret, womblike, organic? Yet it is a threat to women. Men move in it freely and with confidence, they earn their livelihood from it, it is a source of power: may this not reflect the male triumph over matriarchy? Yet why does the grandmother live in the forest? Perhaps she personifies some older order of the organic female link with nature which still survives and could threaten men?

Our story editor has now tilted the play to something more acceptable to a general audience. The story seems solid with plenty of action. There are figures with whom the audience may identify and an object on which they may release their aggression. He has worked out ritual and some rather chic myth. Finally the story is not going to offend anyone, it supports traditional morality, so the audience is not going to have to come to terms with any new ideas, or failing to come to terms with them is not going to have to find rational reasons for their rejection. Well, there it is: efficient in a superficial kind of way.

Another man, not a story editor (that is, not a man brought in to botch up a play and make it acceptable to an audience), might approach the material quite differently. He may start writing something, messing around, enjoying himself; but sooner or later he's going to feel dissatisfied and this feeling will get stronger and stronger until he faces up to what's worrying him, whatever it is. And he will have to stop what he's doing and start groping around trying to discover what his problem is.

I think there is finally only one vital lesson for an artist, but all artists must learn it and it's something they can only teach themselves. It is to know when they are dissatisfied, to know that they must stop because they have lost touch with some central vital thing. An artist must be ready to realise that what he is doing has lost its point and ask himself why. To discover what he is trying to express and then to sense if he has lost touch with it. An artist is always trying for the absolute although I doubt whether he can ever be sure that he has got there. Nevertheless, an artist in pursuing what he conceives to be the truth feels a kind of peace and excitement the nearer he gets to the centre of the problem.

I will now confess that while I earlier invented the character of the story editor in order to demonstrate how not to approach a piece of work, it was quite honestly my own initial approach. But, as always, there came a point when one was dissatisfied with what one was doing, it seemed so superficial, uninteresting and dishonest. And so I had to do what one always has to do: face up to the questions which one hoped one would get by without facing. In the course of this muddled questioning—and it is always muddled because one has to follow false leads and so on—I began to make those creative discoveries one always makes when one demands that one satisfy oneself as regards truth. These discoveries always excite one so much that they give one the energy to carry on, and they give one a line, an inexorable line which dictates the form of the whole work. I must add that this process of questioning goes on until the work is finished, a kind of continuous checking that one is being true to the inner nature of what one is doing.

So perhaps one might begin by asking, How is the wolf to be treated? How is he to be shown upon the stage? As a real wolf—I mean an actual wolf?

Difficult. But consider the parallel of bull-fighting—I believe bull-fighting, whatever its ethics, to be one of the most pure and exciting artistic forms—the depth of the myth, the rigid courtly ritual containing violence and death. But it is the very reality of death in the bullring which makes it non-theatrical. Theatre doesn't deal with absolute reality, it deals with imaginative reality. So no real wolf. Well, then, how are we to treat the wolf?—As he might be in ballet perhaps? A man in costume suggesting the inner experience, the essence of wolfdom? How seriously are we to take the wolf? Is he a comic villain? It would be possible to have him funny and yet a real threat also. All depends on the form of the play, or conversely this problem may decide the form. Perhaps if we know how the wolf is to be treated we shall know the form and style of the play.

We try another point of entry. Why doesn't the wolf seduce Red Riding Hood in the forest—why does he lure her off to gather flowers and then leave her and go looking for the grandmother? There are only two possibilities—either he does seduce her, or there is some really strong reason why he doesn't. If he does seduce her then Red Riding Hood's later behaviour makes her very interesting—if he doesn't, why doesn't he? Is he homosexual? Is she unattractive? Then why did he lure her into the forest in the first place? Is he kinky—preferring very old, possibly dead, ladies—and so lures Red Riding Hood into the forest to get her out of the way?

How can a wolf talk? Because the wolf is an extreme image of a certain type of man.

One can accept that Red Riding Hood couldn't tell the difference between her grandmother and the wolf, although there would have to be a particular reason for it in terms of character which would in turn affect the whole play: Is Red Riding Hood short-sighted? Is she exceptionally stupid? Or is she so shy, so well brought up by that mother of hers that although she notices something wrong she doesn't like to say anything because it wouldn't be polite. Or is it that she actually was seduced earlier in the forest?

What I can't accept at present is Little Red Riding Hood's regurgitation. Either she is eaten—that is seduced, her virginity lost—or not. You can't have it both ways. She can't be seduced and then regain her virginity. The alternative: that she is actually eaten, and then rescued by the woodsman, is only truthful if the woodsman is a figure of magical power—a god or demi-god—someone with power of life and death.

To return to the question of the wolf's leaving her in the forest. Is it that the wolf realises that he can have both girl and grandmother? But why doesn't he seduce Little Red Riding Hood in the forest and then go on to the grandmother? Why does he wait until she gets to the cottage—how does he know she'll come to the cottage?

Right: now comes the leap, and at this point in

thinking it out one gets exhilarated. That's it. That's the falseness in the story. The original story lied to make it's point: the wolf does seduce Red Riding Hood in the forest. Once I accept this, doesn't everything fall into place? She follows the wolf to the cottage and the ritual dialogue takes on quite a different colour and becomes sex play: 'Why grandmother, what big ears you have!'—then follows the second intercourse. It was she who followed him to the cottage, the first time he may have seduced her, the second time she seduces him. When the woodsman arrives Red Riding Hood buys her return into conventional society by betraying the wolf. By her betrayal we begin to recognise that the wolf is the outsider, the outlaw, the hunted man. Now we begin to glimpse the true mythical nature of the situation: the woman rooted in conventionality, who longs for excitement and adventure which her normal environment doesn't give her, she tastes the excitement and danger of consorting with the outlaw. But if she stayed with him she would have to abandon conventional society and she hasn't the courage for that, so she buys her way back into society by misrepresenting what happened—she says the wolf seduced her and this lie is accepted—this is her regurgitation.

This is the myth that Sidney Nolan found so fascinating in his series of paintings of Mrs Frazer and the escaped convict: the conventional woman consorts with the wild man, who in his turn sees in her some promise of the comfort and secure happiness he has lost; when she has had enough and wants to return to her own kind, she turns on him and betrays him.

We have turned Little Red Riding Hood inside out. It started by glorifying women and denigrating men in an unhealthy and inverted way. But it did it by lying about the details of its story. As soon as the lie is exposed one sees that the woman, far from innocent, is the predator and the man is the victim.

Bearing in mind that the artist's view of truth must be coloured by his unconscious, the artist of integrity simply cannot ask himself whether this story would be popular or not, would appeal to women or not. Once he has allowed himself to be gripped by his material the artist must follow the subject where it will go giving it the shape it appears to demand. He cannot manipulate the story, except within very narrow limits, he can only discover its shape. If the story will disturb his audience he cannot help that (indeed disturbing the audience may be his unconscious aim, all artists want to be loved and accepted as much as anyone else, although this desire may take strange forms). The pursuit of truth is so fascinating and inexorable that the artist must follow.

Truth in this context may mean factually truthful, or truthful in terms of the artist's vision—in which case the product may be in fact a lie and insulting to the audience, but it remains a truthful picture of what the artist sees, and will have the valid, absolute quality of artistic truth.

Given a hypothetical great dramatist, this man is theoretically in a delicate position: if he abides by what he sees as truth, produces a truthful piece of work, it is almost certain to disturb his audience, because society—that is the audience—is always tending away from truth and the absolute, which are too uncomfortable to be borne for more than short periods. But if our great dramatist produces a piece of work designed to please his audience at the expense of truth then his work will lack power, and to an artist the power in his work is the whole point of working.

We have seen a situation in which the dramatist hopes that his audience is seduced into surrender by means of an appeal to imagination reinforced by sensual and emotional stimuli; their brains, their rational minds are lulled, their emotions, senses, instincts and memories are assaulted, stimulated, impregnated. It would seem in theory that the audience is defenceless. Receptive and open to any suggestion they must succumb to the artist, the skilful manipulator, who need only apply his technique to brainwash his audience and transform the world.

But art does not change the world much; it only changes the world when the world is ready to be changed. If art is reinforcing something that the audience wants to believe then it may be effective indeed. But by and large art has little direct influence and I think this is because although the artist may call upon the irrational and unconscious forces in his audience those same irrational forces will be their protection. As a general rule, until they get used to a new idea an audience will reject what a dramatist has to say if it challenges their preconceptions. If a play conflicts with certain of my preconceived ideas about art or morals then either I am going to have to reassess my ideas, which is uncomfortable and disturbing, or else I must in some way rob the play of its power.

In theory art has limitless power because so much of its appeal is to the unconscious, and it is the unconscious that rules the world despite the image we have of ourselves as rational beings. And of all the arts the theatre is probably the least resistible, not merely because it makes its appeal to so many facets of our personalities—senses, intellect, emotions—but also because the audience is in a way captive. It is much less easy to walk out of a theatre than it is to walk away from a picture; generally speaking in the theatre you are exposed to the experience from its start to its finish. But brainwashing is one thing, the theatre is another. It is going to take more than an evening's image-making, and more than a little myth and ritual to make us accept something which is at variance with our own fiercely defended unconscious values.

Published by the Syndics of the Cambridge University Press
Bentley House, 200 Euston Road, London, N.W.1
American Branch: 32 East 57th Street, New York, N.Y.10022

PRINTED IN GREAT BRITAIN